Small Talk
& Long Silences

Small Talk
& Long Silences

Michael Riedell

**Slow
Mountain
Press**

Some of the poems in this collection originally appeared in somewhat different form in *Mendocino Arts Magazine* and on *KZYX&Z's Rhythm Running River*.

9 8 7 6 5 4 3 2 1

First Edition

Printed in the United States of America

ISBN 978-0-9979677-0-8

Slow Mountain Press
innisfree@pacific.net
Ukiah, CA

For Susan Sparrow

and

Hal Zina Bennett

Table of Contents

I

II

III

We Americas are trained to think big, talk big, act big, love big, admire bigness but then the essential mystery is in the small.

–*Jim Harrison*

meteors are not needed less than mountains...

–*Robinson Jeffers*

I

Welcome

You know it's a poet's home
by the silence
of a poem being written.

Please, sit, read.
I'll be right with you.

Good to Know

It's nice to know
history is full
of fools like me—

lazy except for scribbling
poetry

Summer Song

A cool, windy morning
        between trees,
the sun stretching up
        intent to please.

A summer full of days
        I'll have like this:
the sun, the mountain,
        and idleness.

Where

Where redwoods stretch to the sky
& blue jays squawk their tune

Where you can smell the neighbor gettin' high
& Kate stirs beans with a wooden spoon

The Hike to the Ridge

From our place you can
hike to the ridge & from there
see clear to the ocean.

I've done it before &
I will do it again. Today, though,
I'm in more of a sittin' mood...

but imagine that view!

Bluegrass in the Redwoods

Bluegrass in the redwoods
yellow daffodils, white
ocean wind on the mountain
lazy day, warm night

Banjo pluck & guitar strum
bass bump & fiddle fire
the sound of waves rolls through the leaves
with songs of loss, songs of desire

Half My Heroes

Half my heroes
           were hobos
The other half
           never left home—

Mossy rocks
           & rolling stones

Mountain Path Triptych

It's hard to tell where
you are on this mountain path—
          Keep moving
          you'll learn

          *

I stop on the path
to write a haiku—
          Such green sounds!
          The mountain's alive!

          *

Dreaming of an old
mountain hermit—
          Just this muddy path
          the wind & me

Light

Hunting mushrooms a week late
in the forest out back,

I push back loam to find only
a battered bolete here

and a moldy matsutaki there
just this side of the huckleberry,

but the sun throws its lifelines
down between the trees.

What a world! I return home
lighter than when I left.

Counterpoint

Two juncos bickering
at a bird feeder—

their frantic dance,
a pianist's hands.

The Gift a Guest Brings

Ah! sweet niece,
wise niece—

She does not ask me,
How is school?
        or
When will dinner be ready?

        but
What kinds of birds do you have?

And then she listens to the answer.

Blue Canoe

Call me the fool
with the silly blue canoe

Say Row, row
your funny little boat
Michael

a-shore, or
off shore
just be sure
to row
that silly blue
canoe
Michael

Row, row
that funny blue
canoe

Swatting Flies

They say Man named all the animals,
and I know words are powerful,
so why not call them

> barn flies,
> jungle flies,
> desert flies,

or stay-the-hell-out-of-my-house flies?

Dust

On the wall hanging
     cliffs & trees

    & a river

like any other
     dirtier each year

Farewell

First scrub jay of the day

    why

        off

           so soon

Indecision

RIP Kona the Wonderdog

All day the dog
stares through the glass door

one side then
the other

Death You Are

Death you are
a mosquito

       buzzin' in my ear
       buzzin' in my ear

a sound that might be pretty
if it weren't so near

The Poet Celebrates His Boon of Mushrooms, Waving Wide the Guide Book

Then he sees, on the opposing page,
another mushroom
identical in color and bulbousness,

but poisonous.

Seventy-Miles Per Hour

Seventy-miles per hour
these days
is so routine,
deer asleep
at the roadside
never bother
to lift their heads
to watch us
streak by.

Mendocino Farmers

These farmers, too, have big trucks,
huge trucks, but lifted too high
for sheepdogs or hay bails, too clean
to want to throw dusty bags
of chicken feed or old fence posts in,

and tricked out with extra lights
and needless chrome that shines
like these farmers spend each day
polishing their trucks to perfection
and not really working at all.

Country Classic

The song that's stuck in my dumb head
will be the death of me—

It's armed with guns (American!)
and shooting its way free.

Revels

More than half drunk

the green bottle
wears a cork
for a top hat

& dances on the table

Glimmers

In the glass coffee table
the birds of glimmers
dart back & forth,
shining off the swinging
chimes outside:

reflections of reflections:
the sunlight & me.

Property

You say you own this land,
these trees, this dirt, & all the stones?

You don't own anything
that can digest your bones.

Interruption

Fog drops,
      the cold,
            a cone falls from a tree—

a slug stops,
      continues
            curiouslessly.

Note to My Boss

I got up with the alarm,
on time,
and went down to make coffee
when she
dragged me back to mate.

Then I was late.

The Crimes of Billy the Kid

He clutched and clawed
        at his chest, shot.

He wobbled, tottered
        and groaned a lot,

then swearing vengeance
        fell dead to the ground.

Yes, children turn men
        into clowns.

Hermit's Saturday Night

Redwoods swing a little
on a Saturday night;

I swing a little
on a Saturday night.

One of us calls it quits first.

Kimono

For robe I have a kimono
whose sleeves are huge
and have secret pockets
big enough I swear to hide
my whole heart in, but

standing at the stove those
sleeves drop into the eggs,
so most often I wear the
soft blue robe my sweet
stepmom-in-law got me,

the one I pulled from
a wrapped box that said
     Meryvn's.

I wear it all winter.
In fact, I'm wearing it now!

Just Listening

Not wise enough
        to be a monk
or seer enough to be a poet

Me, I'm lazy
        and end up like the back porch
just listening to birds

Thoughts While Weeding

Every time I weed it seems
I accidentally pull out plants

I planted as seeds and watered
and grinned to see first sprout.

God, too, I think, sometimes
yanks the wrong person out.

Mendocino Lunch Poems

i

Throw down a jacket for a blanket.
Bring a lunch, bring a book.
Take an hour for yourself and
have a seat under the sun.
Do you need instructions for this?

ii

It took me a full sub sandwich
and half a bag of chips
before I saw it on the beach below me
written with a dragged stick: "Tara was here."
All our poems—what more do we say.

iii

Watching seagulls from here,
it's hard to resist the temptation
of their grace, the urge to jump—
this sea-cliff is so high,
and the blue swell so ready to catch me.

The Winning Horse

The Kentucky Derby was over, and
I'd lost a little money—

but how much
could I have lost really when,

as the winning horse was met
by another horse and rider,

those two horses nuzzled each other,
and I realized victories,

when I do have them, are
nothing without you.

Grapes

Walking with you before dawn,
without streetlights or a moon
to tell us their dull truths,

the clusters of grapes I know
hang dark and full
beside our footsteps are gone,

and the stars above glow so close
it hardly seems a dream to think
of plucking that brightest one
for you to eat.

My Favorite Leaf

My favorite leaf
on the dogwood
so high above
I'll never touch it—

when night arrives
I call it star;
during daylight
I call it crow.

I will never touch it
unless, come autumn,
I turn these hands to rakes
and comb the garden's curls.

So it is to have
a favorite leaf
so high above
in a dogwood tree.

Rereading

Turning a moment
from my book
to look at you—

you are rubbing your
chest, your breast,
so soft and ivory,

lovely, lowering
your collar to rub
further, nearly

to your nipple.
I look back at
my book and then

back to you.

The Day Is Silver and Calls to Us

It's the neighbor boy, Jackson,
stumbling his little legs toward his sister—
      Hey! Hey!

It's a new bird with a strange new cry—
      Haw! Haw!

It's a fawn, wobble-kneed, slow,
behind its mother stretching its neck—
      Here! Here!

In late November rain my wife and I
wrapped in a blanket learn again
      to listen, to see:

The day is silver and calls to us.

Chore-wise

All winter I'm inside
beside the wood stove,
writin' songs & dreamin'
of all the work I'll do
once there's sun...

Then, come spring,
I don't get much done
each day, chore-wise, but it's okay—
out among the trees & my dog
howling up at squirrels
I have my fun.

But Then Who's to Decide, Really?

–for Janice

Putting chains on tires
the night before you need to go

shouldn't feel like such
indulgence–but

the frosted moon, the stars,
the glowing snow!

Hemingway's Matadors

They could have learned
while splitting wood

—the art of arcing body,
        poise,

avoiding knots, finding grain.

Still Reading

The fool
keeps reading
when his eyelids bow
& pray for sleep

I am such a fool

Carrying My Bones: A Winter's Tale

Some days I hardly even leave the house
but mosey from room to room,
carrying my bones like firewood.

I set them on the floor beside the couch
and watch mist slide between tanoaks.
I pick up books and put them down.

At noon eggs cry out to be freed from their shells.
Beginning to understand their restlessness,
I reach for a femur and smash the whole dozen.

The suns of twelve days shine at once!

What the Spider Knows

The spider in the armload
of firewood somehow knows:

The leather sky of my glove
may have missed once but will
descend again.

We run in vain.

Truth Is

Truth is
when I cut the bluster,
cut the shit,

I'm like the lonely mourning dove,
barely making it.

*

Truth Is (Part 2)

When I whisper
to the stars
I say,

We're struggling
here on earth

but
it's worth it.

Dawning

The darkness
between trees
silvers, moves
my dark mood
toward light,
toward life.

II

Impressionable

Whenever those old Chinese nuns leave
Ten Thousand Buddhas and come
into town, I want to follow them
through the Co-op, try
what they buy, switch
to robes, shave
bald as stone,
have a seat
and say
Om.

The Less I Say

Now I'm no scholar, but
　　　I have discovered this:

The Reason that can be reasoned
　　　is not the eternal Reason.
The Way that can be talked about
　　　is not an Unvarying Way.
The truth that may be told
　　　is not the everlasting Truth.
The Dao that can be expressed in words
　　　is not the constant Dao.
The Tao that can be spoken
　　　is not the eternal Tao.

However it's translated, it's clear:

　　　the less I say
　　　the better.

Metaphor

Snoozing at my desk
        I get an idea

A squirrel climbs a tree
        a small branch drops

How a Poem Works

One paper cup
in one hand,

another
in another's,

the string between
pulled tight—

this.

Genuine

From a thought by Marianne Moore

After weeping my way into the world
I was taken to an apartment
on Redwood Avenue
some 400 miles from a real redwood tree,
then was fed milk
that was not my mother's.

I've been searching for the genuine
ever since.

Letter to Judevine Mountain

For David Budbill (1940–2016)

I got ahold of your poems recently
& have been enjoying them, savoring them

slowly: a couple each morning
like eggs to start the day.

Time & space, old Einstein told us, are one
& now, again, I believe:

Thirteen hundred years to the T'ang poets,
three thousand miles to your mountain in Vermont—

Both are impossibly far
& no further than a tea cup.

Thank you for your work, friend,
but don't feel you need to write back.

Han Shan never did.

Simple

I am simple:

This loose faith
in the words
others write,

that I write
almost to them.

This Time Hayden

There's nothing like the death of a great one
to get me back to reading poetry.

I'm never gone long: They drop like flies
that don their cap a last time, pack

up their clarinet, and sometimes
without even a parting glance, fly away, leaving

just these words that buzz
black upon the page.

After a Long Time Away

The Muse is such a sweet and caring hostess—
knock and she answers
every damn time.

But that don't mean
she'll always bring out the fine china
& choicest wine...

Don't sweat it!
& don't complain.

& keep your elbows off the table!

Rain Song

Rain! Rain!
We should be weeping
with joy,

our tears joining
your procession
from the heavens

to the parched and
patient
earth.

Compassion

The great statue
of Kuan Yin on the hill
above flooded Sendai

She must have wept
while
no one was looking

I Would Hold You

I would hold you
like a jar outside
gathers and saves rain
eager for each new drop

I would hold you like a child
with sticky fingers
holds a lollipop
even in sleep

I would hold you like the drowning
hold their breath

Much Like Eskimo Snow

Our bickering
is another language.

Those around us hear
curses and insults;

They do not know
my love and I are playing

at the 7300 ways
our language has

to say
I love you.

Tire Rolling

Rolling old tires
uphill to dump—

Sisyphus, I think of you,
you and the endless

tire-rolling schoolyard
of my youth.

It was fun then,
Fun now.

What's your complaint?

Some Sundays

The only clock worth watching
is the shadow the sun pries
out from under each object
all afternoon—

> bushes, buckets,
> old sheds—

Eastward they crawl
like they just might reach
all the way
to yesterday.

Looking Over Old Poems

So few are written for you to see.
They litter the ground behind me
like bread crumbs from a child's fable
to help the old man I'll become—
legs weak and covered in a quilt—
to recall the steps I once took.

But today, old friend, I brought
sticks and glue and string enough
to make and fly a kite so high
even you can see it, just outside
your window, up there above the trees,
that white speck that hardly seems to move.

That's me, flying a love letter to you.

Silver Dawn

i

Silver dawn & I
read Chinese poems
      so simple

we both think we
could've written them

ii

Silver light
      through the blinds

my wife's sleepy breathing
      then mine

Math

For Sid

They say it's everywhere, and I believe them
in my way—uncritically—
but this morning
standing before the mirror, I see it:

Geometry:

the square of my face, the semi circle
of my skull top, the isosceles triangle
of my bearded jaw above the cylinder
of my neck—a precarious stack,
a child's play
of rudimentary shapes, each seeking its balance
in the whole, each
unaware
of its precise formula.

Grandchildren

No children I'm fine with
but this evening reading
a Chinese translation
mentioning "grandchildren"

I picture myself on the floor
playing cards or pushing cars
with the poems
of my poems

What I Had Done

The tiny white feather was nothing
when it was on me, hardly a nuisance,

but once I flicked it from my sweater,
it found flight and lived, again,

in a moment as slow
and elegant as a swan,

while I wondered what I had done
and if it could be undone.

Dog

I wanted to be a cat
—cool, indifferent—

but the way you look down at me

humping your leg,
I know what I am.

Group Therapy

Sybil and her ilk
have the luxury of relegating pain
to underlings.

The rest of us
dumb-luck schmucks are stuck
carrying the whole load ourselves—

Where's our book?
Where's our movie?

The Elm and the Moon

The houseplant says—

> *I am an elm!*

The golf ball in the pot says—

> *And I am the moon*
> *come down*
> *to rest in your shade.*

Karma

I'm waiting for a huge dinosaur
to come falling through the sky

& crashing to the earth
kill off all the rocks

Friends, Do You Remember

"I remembered all the lands of the Warring Time."
   –Ko Un

Friends, do you remember
back in the day
when we had to march in the streets
just to stop a needless war?

Thank God
they listened.
Thank God
we won't have to do that again.

After Dali's "Le Sommeil"

Unconscious we do seem
to teeter like that yet not fall,

fat-faced, and on such twiggy crutches,
half-deflated as a bounceless ball,

while a dog quite patiently watches
to see what he has for a master:

a god or a goddamned disaster.

First Thoughts at Dawn

"What sense does it make to hand [your] brain to someone
for eight hours a day, for their particular use, on the
presumption that at the end of the day they will give it
back in an unmutilated condition?"
    —Bruce "Utah" Phillips

What a mind we were born with, to wake
just before the alarm, with a pillow
for our head like a gift
brought for a king, capable of such
royal thoughts, though, this morning,
as sometimes happens, the jewel teems
not with butterflies of delight
but gray reflections, the common
drudge of a frustrated serf.

What They Rake For

Bald-headed Zen monks
templed in Japan
rake designs in sand
to bring peace of mind

Mexican peasants
in the sun's bald heat
rake mountains of salt
for a richer man's meat

Gringos on weekends
rake when they can
to keep up appearances
their yards and their tans

My Pet Rock

My pet rock is a failed grenade
It cannot blow my loneliness away

I paint it with a smiley face
But a smiley face can never replace you

I wish I were an Edison
I'd invent a happy ending then be done

Little Girls Across the Street

From out back I hear
the little girls across the street
their high-pitched Spanish chatter
swirling like red leaves in a gale

If I listened well enough
I'd understand some of it
and miss all of what I love about it

I am no scholar
and need no exactitude
Whatever they say
they say

joyfully

When She's Gone

—three poems for Kate

You call!
The world is a blossom.
We hang up.
Wilt.

*

For the colony
an ant will step over dead brethren
with hardly a pause

You're gone a few days
and my knees crack

*

This morning walking
I heard a cackle, thought:
scrub jay!—then, no:
crow, and an old crow it was
in a thin, leaf-lost tree
cackling down
right at me.

He knew you were gone,
sang me his love-loss song.

Coming Close

I used to want to be a hobo,
tramping on trains,
seeing the spreading land.

And I tried being a mountain recluse,
holed up with woodchucks,
seeing into myself.

There's always striving, seeking,
doing the best we can.

Whenever we come close,
it's worth at least a quick grin,
or a kiss, or a poem.

Balance

We speak of finding it
as if it can be found

as if it's hiding in the garage rafters
trying not to make a sound

as if seeking it
were not a lifetime's folly

as if our touch would not disrupt

something so holy

In Praise of the Half Moon

What does it say that this half moon
is my favorite—and this half, not the other.

Strange white mouse ear, hanging there
beside the redwood's silent silhouette,

Can you hear me? Do you hear?

The full moon, yes, is magnificent,
and the new moon's humility

makes a whole night of stars, but this
half moon, I choose her most to love.

Waving

Leonard Cirino, 1943-2012

Up here high on the mountain
the tanoak leaves wave like
ten thousand fans, like
ten thousand hands of schoolgirls
lined up along a parade route.

These trees know when a poet is passing.

Six A.M. Poem

You'd think I think
a stairway to heaven could be
built with used books.

You'd think getting going
on that construction must be
why I wake so damn early.

Wrong, wrong.
Everything I do I do
to help breed these little poems—

and I don't kid myself
they'll get me anywhere

but here.

Crackers

Some poems slip
through the cracks
like a cracker tossed
to the dog on the back deck—

it may have vanished
but we know it's there
by the dog's
desperate sniffing.

Notice

If a poem should come to you,
out of nowhere,
it's mine.

I lost it.

Just a while ago
I went to write it,
and it was gone.

You'll know it if you find it.

If it comes to you,
it's mine.

And it's not good to steal.

Question with a Cow's Eye

If the eye of a cow were a planet
& its cornea a continent, lush & restful,

where one afternoon beside a quiet brook
you lay daydreaming of cirrus clouds
& blue-winged songbirds—

if I were to happen upon you, gentle, strong,

would it be love?

Tasting the Rainbow

We decide a rainbow
would taste like fruit—
cherry, mango,
honey-dew melon.

What about the blue?

I look into her
almost six year old
blueberry eyes
while she imagines it.

The Snail

So slow
the snail
after I
water well
the garden—

Where, friend,
tell me where
do you go
so slowly
and why?

This wet walk
is trod
by feet that move
too fast
for you

(too fast
even for ourselves).

Down

I'm down to a cup
of coffee, cold, and

not the moon but
the idea of the moon

just outside the blinds
ready to be found

at dawn, hanging
pale and half.

White Roses

If the roses on the kitchen table are white
and the morning is only just breaking
into birdsong and light,
and if I am alone at that table,
know this:

You are on my mind.

Whatever dreams
may be teeming in your head,
you are on my mind.

Hot Tea

She is sick.
Drinking the hot tea I brought her,
she says,

> *It feels good to burn my throat.*

I want to say it's like blasphemy,
but what do I believe?

> I will not speak against this:

Sunday morning
in bed
in love.

If I Were Another

After Mahmoud Darwish

If I were another, I'd—
        No.
Today I'm too wise for such folly,
        even in a poem.

If I were another, you
        wouldn't love me.
No one can hope for such luck
        twice.

Realization

The birds in my throat
that ad lib their morning songs
have flown away

with my dog.

A Gift of Strawberries

I can't hand an old lady beggar woman
strawberries from the too big basket I bought
for breakfast in Paris without thinking
of how much longer she might have
to live.
      Death in the catacombs beneath us,
death on my mind all the time.

I ought to be ready when the old hand is mine.

Poem to Ukiah

Written on October 20th, 1999, two months
after I first came to these valleys and 17 years
before being named Ukiah's 7th Poet Laureate

Between the gone
        and return
of students
        blind to the sun
I rest under,

        Ukiah,
admiring your gold
        and green
mountains, I swear
        I would die
pleased having been
        your voice,

but when I go
        I won't return:
mountains lead
        to other mountains;

rivers find the sea.

Whatever Poetry's Worth

For Ron Ford

I found South Carolina, "The Palmetto State,"
less humid & backwoods than I figured it,
more round & silver like every other quarter.

I'd been walking while reading a poem
& discovered, whatever poetry's worth,
distraction's worth 25 cents more.

Moth

This little white moth—
he never tires of fluttering the window.

Move on, friend,
move on!

III

Small Talk

Small talk
       & long silences–

fire crackles

   *

Small talk
       & long silences–

Another cup of tea?

Tracing Circles

My fingertips
trace circles on her back

the cycles
of ten thousand years
roll by

A Common Grain

There's a tree I've been circling
as I drive & hike & dream, though

what kind of tree or where
it stands I do not know.

It's wind-whipped & drought-plagued—
a member of an ancient wood—

but its rings pulse out from my source, too;
our heart-woods share a common grain.

The Good News of Our Grand Evolution

The good news of our grand evolution
through mud to this isn't the stardust

in your eyelashes, but that the bitterness
of a six year old in a hurry still struggling

to tie his second shoe will someday be
Lao Tzu wisdom and perfect contentment

every moment of every day, minds that shine
as clear and bright as our stardust eyes.

Greetings

Good morning, book reader!

> Country lane,
> farmhouse porch.

Good morning, bike rider!

> Blue sky,
> quiet breeze.

Good News Right Now

Yes, friends, it is

a time of rancor
        & displacement
of plastic idols
        & fallen monuments

but have you seen

      snow
       on
     madrone?

Touch

Two pairs
      of leather gloves
            that stone wall tore up—

now snow sits on it

     without a care

Again Sendai

For/From Sam Hamill

"From the Chinese shih,
poetry is the word for word
married to the word for temple,
the temple a pictograph of the hand
reaching down, cradling a seeding."

On my quiet mountain
I read and remember
again Sendai,
the temple I wept in
looking up at a painting
of a beggar whose hand reached up
holding forth

       an empty bowl.

Discovery

Here together on the couch—
      my feet in your armpit, yours in mine,
      a blanket over us—

I wonder
      is this how, so long ago, Yin & Yang
      were first discovered,

that opposites could fit so well,
      that there can be a place
      for everyone's

      cold toes.

This Bit of Pollen

Could this bit of pollen
floating
      slowly
           down
have been blown into orbit
by me
      with a wish
a thousand lives ago?

Beside Her Lingering

"Did you lie beside her lingering in the waking hour?"
—Gordon Black

Not often, or
not often enough, certainly,
but this morning, yes, I lingered long,
till a while after noon,
        talking, laughing, napping,
        rolling around together and—

But yours is a yes or no question.

Did I linger beside my love, my wife?
        Yes! Yes!

And some people hope to find heaven
in the next life...

From the Big Bang to Backyard Miracles

Consider even a simple carrot

    bursting from the earth
      so greenly up

    burrowing so
      orangely down

Ocean Wind

The ocean wind way up here on the mountain
my mind down along the shore

The wind this time of year sure is something
a tide-pool sky, ebb and flow

Today's Wisdom

We know what we know
      We lack what we lack

We work in kitchens
      Where dishes crack

Reprieve

Celebrating Buddha's death day
a day late

      after all these years—

mockingbird mocks me
dove coos
      it's okay

He Loves Me

For Ben

While Daddy's at work
Mommy teaches their little girl
    He loves me–
    He loves me not
using purple pansies....

The spring breeze!
The sun!
So many pansies!

She screams,
    He always loves me!

House Fly Sutra

When the fly landed
below the word
    Love
it seemed to be
      reading.

Then it rubbed
its hands together
    as if
to warm them over
the fire of the word,
    or
to prepare to pray,

but then it
flew away.

House Warming

We arrived with brushes
and yellow paint.

Seeing that, the daffodils
came to greet us.

Relocation

Did I trade a whole mountain
    for more blue sky?
Did I leave the green forest
    to give this garden a try?

Yes, yes,
    but I brought my best friend.
And yes,
    I would do it again.

Another Idle Song

"mind and water
both pure idleness"
–Li Po

Work if you wish, friends
I'll sit out here
     idle as a birdbath

between a frog's need to be heard
and a finch's nearly
     silent sipping

Hot Tub Laughter

Late night
     hot tub laughter
floating like
     steam above

I've slipped &
     hit my head
& drowned in
     love again

Them Buddhas

The man handing me
back my change
down at the corner store
—for beer—
had the beard
and few words
of a Buddha...

I realize this
back here
reading about Li Po
and Tu Fu
meeting at a country
wine shop.

Them Buddhas
are everywhere
once you start looking.

Silk Tree Reverie

I have Japanese calendars
with silk trees just like this one—

silver dusk to frame it,
hummingbird still making rounds.

Those others are boxed up inside;
I'll take this one.

Moon Walk

Me & my dog
a country road
& a big ol' moon

We'll head home
I guess
pretty soon

Your Faith

The oak tree does not
need your faith

The blue jay does not
need your faith

The winter sun knows well
who to love

All-Saints Day

Yesterday we were
whatever we wanted to be—goblins,
witches, hobos, Harry Potters.

Today we are all saints.

Straighten your halo.

Glow.

Violet Sunset

There's a yellow moon
watching a violet sunset
a little girl beside me
with her hand in mine

I don't know
what the divine is up to, but
keep up the good work
I'm doing fine

Holy Water

How holy water
got in the bird bath
I don't know—

But those robins
sure like splashing in it!

Acceptance

Today I begrudge the world
of nothing—its hurricanes
of pollen, the flooded gutters
where leaves swirl in dirty eddies,
even the travails of teenage girls.

Today I am open to it all.

Spin, sweet world!
Silly world,
spin!

This Sparrow

God isn't a poet
like this sparrow
whose whistle
wakes the air

God *is* this sparrow
is the whistle
is the air

Riverbank

I held my breath
like a smooth stone in my hand
where I knelt beside a silence
as graceful as a river.

When I threw my stone in
I didn't expect a splash—
such a strangely
noiseless little splash!

If I Hold You

If I hold you
And the sparrow holds you
And the sun holds you
And the golden mulberry leaves of autumn
         hold you too

You do not need to choose among us
You do not need to choose

Let This Poem

Let this poem gather moss.
Let rain bead and drip from this poem,
Find its way to creek and wherever that might lead.

Let this poem stay here
With only the touch of deer hoof to disturb it.

Seed Poem

The wind, the wind
spins down and
around in spirals
the silk tree's pods,
a strange cloud
of tan-brown
spinning pods like
DNA, I think,
and then I think—
    Yes! Yes,
DNA indeed!
So the wind
helps the tree,
so the warm wind
spreads the seed
that holds the code
of life, that flows,
too, through me.

Breathing

The first breath
is for the living.

The second is
for those who have gone.

The third is in recognition
that we'll all go too.

And then the breathing
begins again.

How Much Better

I want to say
how much better *it* is,

but really it's
how much better *I* am

when the hand the fly lands in
isn't half a clap

but a pedestal,
and the fly

becomes a tiny
masterpiece,

iridescent
and green!

Excess

One more
maple leaf
and the lawn

I think
would be less
perfect

Then one
falls and
no

Leaves Leaves Leaves

Leaves above, leaves
        on the ground, leaves
                behind my eyes

all of them quivering
        just to be
                just to be alive

Maple Watching

If I could only watch that maple, only
that little Japanese mountain maple
we inherited from Kate's grandpa—

all the turns of leaf and branch and color
throughout the day and year—

I think I could learn something, maybe not
enlightenment, exactly,
but something good.

Then a chattering jay shoots past
and I'm back to
happily distracted again.

Acknowledgements

Tremendous thanks to Susan Sparrow and Hal Zina Bennett for their early and steady support, faith, and friendship.

Thanks to the many poets whose work has influenced my own, especially T'ao Ch'ien (365-427), also known as Yuan-ming, whose poem "Substance, Shadow, and Spirit" helped suggest the organization of this book—however poorly I followed it.

Thanks to Chris Douthit for his wise editorial advice.

And thanks to Kate, my wife, my toughest editor, and my best friend. All my love.